A
Citrus
Kind
of Love

A
Citrus
Kind
of Love

Nymeria Publishing, LLC

First published in the United States of America by
Nymeria Publishing LLC, 2022

Copyright © 2022 by Emmett Ferree

Nymeria Publishing
PO Box 85981
Lexington, SC 29073

Visit our website at www.nymeriapublishing.com

ISBN 979-8-9851572-2-2

Printed in U.S.A

For Ayden, with love.

Table of Contents

A Citrus Kind of Love

"Defenseless."

"What?" I shielded my eyes from the sun and watched as he made his way across the yard.

"This orange," he replied, sitting down next to me. He sunk his teeth into the fruit and slowly took its fragrant flesh into his mouth. "It's defenseless. It had no say when it was plucked from the tree, thrown onto the supermarket display, and ultimately splayed across the cutting board on the kitchen counter."

I shook my head. "It's a piece of fruit. It grows on a tree, we pick it, and then we eat it."

"Precisely. It serves a purpose. And we serve a purpose, too. Humanity exists, but why?"

"Because we evolved?"

He nodded. "Yes, that we did. But why?"

"To get ahead?"

"Why?"

"I don't know," I sighed and leaned against the rough siding of the garden shed. "It's an orange, and I'd rather think of it as an orange, not some grand philosophical discussion."

"Okay, but think about it for a second—what if we evolved to be exactly like an orange? To live only to be consumed, taken advantage of, disregarded?" He took the final orange slice between his teeth, pulling on the flesh before carefully discarding the rind. "I mean, at the basic biological level, we exist to procreate, do we not? We exist to progress a specific set of desirable genetics and let the outliers die off. But if something happened—say, a meteor strike or a nuclear explosion—and we suddenly found ourselves on the same level as oranges, what would we become? Would it be considered an evolution or a devolution?"

I stared at the meticulously stacked rinds in the grass. He had a funny way of thinking about things, but it wasn't funny in a bad way. He was an old soul, as his family always said; an old soul with not enough time to ponder everything there was to ponder. Some days that reminder hurt a little more than usual. Today was one of those days.

"Your turn," he placed his hand on my thigh, pulling me away from my thoughts.

"To do what?"

"To tell me what you think of this orange."

He leaned over and kissed me, his lips lingering on mine long enough for me to taste the sticky sweet juice.

He pulled away and smiled. "Well?"

"I'm not sure if I got a good enough taste." I moved over to his lap and straddled his legs, pressing my forehead against his. "Can I have another?"

He grinned. "Be my guest."

I planted my lips on his once more, resting my forearms on his shoulders. He wrapped his arms around my waist and held me tightly against his chest as he leaned back onto the side of the shed. We stayed like this for what seemed like an eternity—it was as if the rest of the world disappeared in this moment, and I was surrounded only by love. It was a warm love, a tangy-sweet citrus kind of love that could only be found in the summer shade, but it was perfect.

"Hey," he whispered, drawing in a slow, deep breath.

"Yes?"

"I think it would be a devolution."

"What?"

"I think it would be a devolution if we were to be like oranges."

"And why's that?" I smiled, brushing the hair away from his eyes.

"Because I wouldn't be able to do this," he lifted the hem of my shirt over my head and tossed it onto the ground beside us. In a single, swift motion, he grabbed my hips and rolled onto the grass where his body hovered over mine.

"I think you're right," I giggled.

He winked. "I know. I'm always right. But there's still one more thing I need to figure out."

"Oh, really?"

"Mm-hm," he leaned in and pressed his chest against mine. "I need to figure out if you're sweeter than that orange."

I touched two fingers to his chest and gently trailed them down to his waist, pausing when I reached his belt. "I guess we'd better get to work then," I whispered. "This might take a while."

He stole a quick glance around the yard before turning back to me. "I've got time," he said, brushing my hand aside. He briefly fumbled with his belt before unhooking the buckle. "I've got all the time in the world."

Not a Love Story

This isn't a love story, or maybe it was.

Maybe it's more like a eulogy—
memorializing the days we wanted
but were never lucky enough to receive;

if this was a love story,
I'd like to think you'd still be here with me.

Loose Threads

I tore my jeans this morning;
it was just a small tear,
a pull
on a loose thread
by the knee
that snagged on the corner
of the kitchen cupboard,
but I felt as if my entire day
unraveled
the same way that thread
unraveled
and left behind a hole
in the denim.

I often feel
as if I am hanging
by a thread,
by the same small thread
yanked loose
by the cupboard door,
and now I can't help but wonder
what holes would be left
when my last string
finally comes loose.

How to Write a Tragedy

You asked me out in the poetry section
of a used bookstore, the words stumbling
from your lips like poorly translated verse,
your native tongue not used to the foreign meter
of love; it was supposed to be a dare.

The guys on your soccer team wanted to know
if I was a dyke or just ugly,
and they sent you find out because hazing
is never supposed to backfire,
but I had been in love with you
since I was seven years old.

I was sat on the floor, pouring over every page
of every book I could reach, absorbing each reckoning,
learning what it meant to live life and feel alive—
it all made sense the moment you sat beside me
and stared into my eyes.

With you, I understood what it felt like
to be at peace, to breathe and feel my heart
beat to the rhythm of a new hope, to feel
the meter of a love song perfectly in tune;
I knew I belonged with you.

Every year I return to that shelf and close my eyes
just to relive the first time I heard somebody else
stutter; I listen to the sound of your voice
and strain my memory as to not forget
what the language of love sounded like
on your tongue—

I never wanted our story to become a tragedy.

Germinate

Beautiful moments
sprout from seeds
rooted in pain
and watered with tears;

after all,
how would we know
what happiness feels like
if it didn't hurt
to begin with?

Lover's Regret

You have been sick for thirteen years.

A broken heart, you say,
and a bruised conscience,
but you have the most beautiful soul;
I can see it within the galaxies
inside your eyes.

They're a kaleidoscope of colors
and stars, of big dreams and grandiosity,
of so much love
that they overflow with tears
because you have so much to give—

I wish I had so much to give,
had something to give—

I wish I had something to teach me the difference
between giving and grieving,
because the thesaurus keeps telling me
that they share the same thing:

      regret.

And I don't ever want to regret loving you,
even though you're sick,
even though you're dying,
even though there's a million galaxies
within your eyes
that we will never get to explore.

All I want is to be happy,
and I want that happiness to be you.

Scam Artist

Anyone who claims that my life is a scam
has never been tricked by beauty, lured by lust;
never had their heart ripped from their chest
and fed to the monsters who lurk
in the shadows, cackling, licking
the blood of desire from their lips.

Anyone who claims that my life is a scam
has never fallen in love.

Buoyancy

It was as if he bathed in ice,
slept in the freezer,
and had glaciers for eyes.

They were the clearest green,
a frosted mint halo
around his pupils—

his eyes held the only color
left in his body,
unless you counted the blue tinge
that lingered on his lips.

It was as if someone sucked the color right out of him,
washed him in ink, bathed him in toner;

I was thirteen when I learned firsthand what a dead body looked like.

I'll never forget the way
the paramedics pulled my father
from the bathtub,
hoisting him up like a ragdoll
and draping his body
across a gurney.

Now I can't even put ice cubes in my water.

I can't watch them bob up and down,
floating on the surface, belly-up
like the night I found my father
after he finally found God.

Scars

It was a car crash, a cat scratch, a shark attack,
a mix of believable unbelievability and absurdity
and a few outright lies, but eventually they stopped asking.

You always wore yours with

       pride,

faded purple lines streaked down your chest—
you spoke of them like you were speaking of trophies,
of victories seemingly unattainable, of captured
and recaptured wealth and health, of a future suddenly bright
because your blood once ran from those coveted wounds
since scabbed over and healed.

Mine were, are, and will forever and always
be shrouded in shame. Why do you do it,

they ask,   you ask,   I ask—

       Why do I do it?

Why does the stroke of a blade, of a razor,
of a broken paperclip, of anything
with an edge to take away my edge
as it's dragged across my skin
seem to bring me relief?

       Does it bring me relief?

It brings me silence, a brief moment
where the world stands still,
where the release of my breath

echoes,   lingers,   dissipates

in front of my face as the next inhalation
of fate rattles me awake

and the thoughts of

>   oh fuck,
>   oh shit,
>   I shouldn't have done this

begin to flood my mind.

You were proud of yours, scared of yours,
at times unaware of yours,
and sometimes I got so angry at you
for having the audacity to run
your fingers over those thickened purple lines
without so much as flinching—

I hated you for being able to touch them
without having to hold back the urge to vomit.

I hated you for knowing yours would fade
while mine would forever remain the same,

>   bloodied,
>   half-scabbed,
>   picked away at;

I hated you for loving mine when I never could.

Pottery

My mother had a vase in the living room,
one she sculpted when I was a child.
I remember watching her hands
quietly coax the wet clay
until it took form; her fingers danced
around the edges, a delicate caress
as she hummed Mozart and Stravinsky
under her breath.

She had a makeshift kiln in the garden
that she baked pottery in every Friday night.
I'd sit in the garden and play
while she drank sweet tea
and read Danielle Steel
and waited for the vases to be done.

Watching her glaze pottery
was one of my favorite things;
seeing that soft enamel sheen
that dried to a light turquoise
and shone in the afternoon sun—
this is the first memory of magic
that I have.

She always kept roses in that vase,
baby pink and yellow, sometimes white,
and sat it in the old bay window.

The movers broke that vase
during our move from Chestnut to Bridgeway,
dropping the box on the front step
and shattering the vase into a thousand shards
alongside my mother's broken heart.

We tried to fix it,
but the bottom always leaked slow, fat tears
that stained a ring onto the coffee table

in the great room.
Now it only holds fake roses,
ones with plastic stems and polyester petals
that do nothing
but wear thin and collect dust.

Gifts

I tried giving you the world
and the sun
and the moon
and the stars
and you repaid me with the galaxy
neatly wrapped and tucked
beneath my eyelids
so I can see your smile
every time I close my eyes
and think of your voice

Gambling Debt

I remember, faintly, a time
when climbing into bed
didn't feel like a game of Russian roulette,
where closing my eyes and resting my head
against the pillow
didn't prompt dreams of being buried alive,
of being left to die, choking
on my own spit inside a coffin
fifteen inches too short.

I used to feel like the weight of the world
was upon me, crushing me,
but now that weight
feels so much
like the blankets atop my chest,
slowly smothering me in my sleep,
inching closer and closer to death
every time I count sheep.

Street Signs

The sign on the corner of Oak and Chestnut
is still crooked
from the time that drunk driver crashed
head-first into the metal post.
It was the first time something like this had happened—
one of the few small-town perks, I suppose—
and nobody seemed all that bothered
by a street sign bent forty-five degrees
at the side of the road.

I had watched the firemen
pull the driver from the car that night,
limb by limb;
they said the guy's left leg
was in the back seat
and the right was on the dash.

I never understood why people
would drink and drive,
drink and die,
but I can't even walk on that side of the street
without seeing a gurney full of limbs
and a dead man's empty stare
reflected in the glare of headlights on the street sign.

Blasphemy

They called it blasphemy—
the way our lips

        touched

the way your fingertips

        caressed

my cheeks,
trailing along my

        skin,

dancing
across my torso,

        undressing

my body,   my desire,   my sins—

they called it blasphemy
because they never knew what

        love

could look like
outside of heterosexuality

and abuse.

Fruit Baskets

Nobody goes to the market for damaged goods,
but everybody comes home
with a few bruised bananas
or peaches or apples
that get left at the bottom of the basket
until they become too soft to handle.

Can you imagine getting thrown away, tossed aside
because the taste of your syrupy love
is too sweet to stomach?

The Baptism

The water burned,
a chill that seared my skin
as the preacher sent me under
to cleanse me of my sins
so my mother could pretend
that my past was left behind
and stored inside
the old baptismal font.

It felt a bit like drowning—
his hands holding me under
a few seconds longer than necessary
to remind me
of the secrets I kept
and the silence he placed upon me,
to remind me
of the body he placed upon me,
to remind me
of the scars and the pain he placed upon me.

Sometimes I think
that my mother wishes
I would have stayed under
a few seconds longer
so she wouldn't feel so bad
about keeping me quiet.

And sometimes I think
that I should have opened my mouth—
not to scream but to drown,
to fill my lungs
with the frigid flames of religiosity—

Do you think somebody
would have finally listened
to me?

True Love

I am not sure
if I have ever truly noticed
how the grass dances with the wind,
how each blade sways its hips
and flows within the wind's embrace—

When I was a child, I would stand atop my father's feet and dance the night
away. He would hold my hands as I balanced my toes on his, giggling as we
rocked back and forth. He would sing to me, telling me I could be whatever I
wanted and that I would always make him proud.

> Father, could I have been a dancer?
> Could I have been a dancer
> like the grass on a sunny spring afternoon?

You see,
I'm beginning to fall for the way the wind
keeps an unspoken promise to the grass;
each blade knows it will have its turn,
each blade knows that the wind's arms
are long enough, are loving enough
to hold and caress each and every one of them
without picking favorites.

My father never picked favorites except for when it came to the old rocking
chair that sat out on the front porch. But even then, he only picked once. He
sanded and stained his rocking chair every summer, whistling to the sweet
tobacco smoke as it spiraled up from the butt of his cigar. His hands would
push and pull away a year's worth of wear and tear, the sandpaper's grit
smoothing the seat's surface just enough to welcome another layer of lacquer.

> Would you have loved me the way my father loved that chair?
>
> Would you have loved me endlessly,

wholly, and beautifully
despite my imperfections?

Would I have been your favorite?

Lovesick

Have you ever felt the fear that comes along with falling in love?

The anxiety that tugs at your heart,
knots your stomach, makes you wonder
if you're even worth the love you long to give—
it's the kind of fear that keeps you awake at night,
tracing the shadows with your eyes in search of monsters,
but the only monsters hiding beneath your bed
are the same ones hiding behind your heart.

Falling in love is the scariest thing I have ever done.

When I met you, I knew you were the one. You were special. You had the
softest voice—a quiet countermelody against the sounds of war—and your
touch was gentle but firm. The way you made me feel safe was genuine,
sweetly secure, and I would give anything to have that back again.

The scariest part of falling in love with you was knowing it would end but not
knowing when.

And when it did end, when I woke up to an empty bed
and you weren't in the kitchen making tea,
when you weren't in the easy chair
with the newspaper and a pastry,
I began to notice all the little things
that were missing, taking note of their absence
as if collecting their shadows would fix me.

Within the first day I found
one less plate at the dinner table,
one less jacket on the coat rack,
one less pair of boots by the door,
one less toothbrush on the bathroom sink—

I was drowning in the emptiness
but it was never enough to make the heartache

go away, so I went to bed,

night after night, gasping for air,
praying that I'd wake up next to you instead.

Distance

I don't know when   I love you
became   love you

or when   sweet dreams
changed to   night

but what I do know
is that I'm scared for the day

when   see you later
becomes   goodbye

Aftertaste

It's how kissing you
feels a little bit like nostalgia
and regret—
like the sweetest sliver of candy floss
dissolving on my tongue
gone two seconds too soon.

It's a shame, mourning the absence
of something I yearn for
while knowing it'll most certainly kill me
in the long run.

But it still feels a little bit like comfort—
a toothache I can't help but prod;
it's almost as if the little moments of pain
seem so good
because the ache reminds me
that it's still possible to feel.

It hurts, yes, but it's something—
and I remember when that something
used to feel like home.

Repentance

We always say forgive and forget,
never discussing forgive and regret,

never discussing whether it's possible
to forgive in the first place—

how do you destroy a monster without becoming one in the process?

Tax Season

I've been told that nothing in this life is guaranteed
with the exception of death and taxes,
and I suppose that is true.

Over the years, I have come to regard death
with a bitter kind of fondness, a sadness
I have learned to love and admire from a distance.

But while the familiarity of death
has etched itself into my skin
to remind me of its inescapability,
I can say with complete certainty
that I still have no clue how to do
my own taxes, and I worry that my life
is committing a fraud too heavy
to take with me to the grave.

Attic Space

The boxes made the attic feel like a wonderland—
cardboard chapels and hospitals
and schoolyards
stood proud against the walls;
dust coated their aging roofs
like a fresh blanket of snow
in a quaint little town
frozen
in a moment of nostalgia.
In this town I could be anything
and anyone
I wanted to be,
so I was a banker, doctor,
lawyer, veterinarian,
and grocery store clerk
every evening after dinner.
The traffic in this town was never a blister
and I never had to wait in line
to buy a soda or a candy bar.
In fact,
I could sit in the old rocking chair
and look out across the entire town square
and not a single soul would pass me by.
Sure, it was lonely at times,
but I was never afraid
to walk the streets alone after dark,
and I would stay out past curfew seven days a week.
The town is different now—
old, deserted,
and most of the buildings
have since been demolished—
but the streets still sound the same
and it still feels a little bit
like home.

Communion

He talked about food like he was talking about God—
spoke about the yolk
running from the center of a perfectly poached egg
as if it was the blood of Christ dripping from a crucifix.
He found his faith through cooking,
found Jesus in the warped reflections
on the bottom of an old copper kettle,
and he baptized himself with white wine every Thursday evening
when he locked himself away to worship.

He went to church less towards the end of his days,
often forgetting to turn off the stove and neglecting to say grace.
He said he couldn't hear the angels anymore,
that he'd tuned out the screams of the tea kettles,
and that he could no longer taste the teachings
he once delivered from psalm to palm every evening.

His pulpit wasn't traditional—
butcher block and granite seasoned with patience
and acceptance and love, real love—
but his sermons were the only thing
that restored whatever connections to God remained.

I've only taken Communion once since he died;
I cried into the wine and saw his face in the ripples
from where my tears broke the surface.
His eyes were tired, but I understood,
placed the chalice to my lips,
and drank as if this bitter sweetness was going to bring him back to me.

Keepsakes

I found a stone by the river,
smooth with streaks of bluish grey.
I sat it on my bookshelf next to the pressed daisies
you gave me the first time you said
I love you.

From the Column of Unwanted Advice

Someone once told me that life would be easier
if I was happier,
that all I had to do
was convince myself that I was fine,
that all I had to do was look in the mirror
and smile so hard that the grin
would never leave my lips.

But that's easy for someone to say, isn't it?

Easy for a person to say when they
aren't constantly watching their loved ones die
and having to live with the pain of knowing
they never got the chance to say goodbye.

Ladders in the Sky

When I was little, I thought there were ladders in the sky, tall and wooden with at least a hundred rungs that carried angels the whole way up to the clouds and beyond the stars. Back then, one hundred was the biggest number I could think of—a hundred dollars was enough to buy the universe, and a hundred minutes felt like the rest of my life. Now, a hundred minutes feels like barely enough time to catch my breath and a hundred dollars isn't much more than a few pennies in an empty pocket.

Where did those days go,
those days that were filled with wonder—
my tiny awestruck eyes took everything in
as if the stars in the sky
were the most beautiful thing I'd ever seen
but would never get the chance
to see again—

And what happened to the days where everything was so beautiful? I used to think my mother looked exactly like a princess and my father was the knight in shining armor that swept her up in his arms and carried her away on horseback.

I don't quite remember when I stopped seeing my mother as a princess, but my father has been dead twenty years now and I can only begin to imagine what his armor would look like today.

This morning I thought about those ladders again—
I sat beneath the sycamore
and tried to figure out just how many rungs I'd need
to make it to the moon.

I stopped counting when I figured out that 784 rungs would only get me to the top of that toy store my mother and I visited when we went to New York.

784 rungs—

That would have taken me to outer space when I was a child.

I could have hopped between asteroids and danced across the Milky Way and painted my face with glitter from the stars; now it barely takes me fifty stories high, and I can only dream of touching the sky while I sit beneath the sycamore and wait for the sun to set so that I can maybe see the stars for just one more night.

Slumber

Last night I
slept

in a bed
that wasn't

mine

and it felt
amazing.

Outerwear

He had a corduroy jacket
the color of melted toffee.
The inside was off-white and wooly—
not a scratchy wooly
but a soft wooly—
and it smelled of pine smoke
and autumn leaves.
He wore that jacket everywhere
with old blue jeans and carpenter's boots;
he looked just like his grandpoppy did
before the war.

We went camping once—
him, his grandpoppy, and me—
and it was beautiful.
He and I slept in a tent beneath the stars
and made love
to the rhythm of the cicadas.
His lips tasted like whiskey
and Lucky Strikes,
and it felt as if I made a lucky strike of my own
every time his skin pressed tight
against mine.

We buried his grandpoppy's ashes six months later
in a coffee tin under the red oak
where I laid on that corduroy jacket,
pressed against the cool earth,
inhaling the scent of pine smoke
and summer sex
and wondering whether or not that moment
was ever going to end.

Fuck

Fuck you. Fuck me. Fuck the world.

Fuck the way this word falls from my mouth, gritty
like the sand between my teeth
and my toes and my trunks
and anywhere else sand shouldn't be
after a day at the beach
where I didn't even want to be to begin with.
I fucking hate the beach.

I didn't always hate the beach.

Fuck, there I go again—

Feeling.

Return to Sender

He wrote me a love letter
seven years ago
and I am still afraid
to open it.

Peaches and Cream

If peaches could sing,
would their songs be as soft and supple
as their flesh? A sugary melody,
each note dripping, sticky sweet,
with tones of warmth and happiness
and summertime sunsets.

What about strawberries—
each bite a burst of love that lingers on my lips
long enough to let me reminisce;
what would they say if they one day had the chance
to spill the secrets that blossomed on their vine,
ripe with everything they've seen and heard?

I often wonder what citrus voices would sound like,
wonder if their voices would sound like mine;
would they be bitter with biting undertones that slip past puckered lips?
Or would they be a gentle refreshment that rolls off the tongue,
smooth and ice-cold against the summer heat?

Apples and apricots, too,
would sing their soprano songs
as cherries and pears join in for a brief cadenza,
a symphony to float through the leaves of the trees
in the warm summer breeze.

If peaches could sing—
if oranges and clementines and all the fruit
from the bushes, trees, and vines were given a voice with
which they could speak as they pleased—

Would they choose to sing only to me?

Or would they sing freely, indiscriminately,
serenading all who pass by
with their sweet summer songs

until the last harvest is done and the final fading melody disappears behind the evening's setting sun?

P.S. I Love You

I will carry the weight of the world
on my shoulders
as long as that weight
is you

Man in the Moon

It was untouchable—
shrouded in intrigue and painted
with the unknown, but it glowed so beautifully
against the starless night sky.

It peeked through the clouds drifting by,
reminding me of when
my mother would brush aside
the locks of hair that danced over top of my eyes.

I used to believe
that if I could touch the moon,
all of my dreams would come true,
like peering into a magic crystal ball
and unlocking every secret to every heartbreak
and hearing the true meaning of happiness
whispered into my ear.

I don't see the moon too often these days;
the sky is cloudy,
and I don't have the best view
from my corner window.

But I still believe
that all my dreams would come true
if I could touch the moon,
because it would be like touching you, too.

Tenancy

I've been living a life of borrowed breaths—
a tenant in a body
that will never be my home;
month after month I pay rent
to an unforgiving landlord,
wishing that one day this house will be mine to own.

I used to think
that this space could be beautiful,
that some new drapes and a fresh coat of paint
would turn this house into a home,
but it's damn near impossible
to fix water damage that has seeped this deep
into the foundation
without tearing everything apart.

Now I'm beginning to think
it might not be worth it,
that a For Sale By Owner sign
outside by the drive would be best,
but I'm worried that I may have to settle
for boarding up the doors and windows
when the power is cut next time I'm late on rent.

Distant Relatives

The rafters in my grandmother's old farmhouse
looked as if they could hold the weight
of the entire world.

And I guess that was true, in a way,
because they held the weight
of my uncle's sins
the night he tied a rope around his neck
and stepped right off the catwalk.

Angel Wings

The morning was dismal—
rain pelted the windows like a battalion of sadness,
soldiers shedding their tears in a spray of bullets
that sought out innocent targets to drown in misplaced agony.

Silhouettes of angel wings
could almost be seen amidst the clouds
scattered across the bleak grey sky,
but I knew those wings belonged to the angels of death.

I had found myself in church that morning.

Found was a strong term, perhaps,
but I thought that something in the Communion wine
would bring me closer to you,
as I couldn't bring myself to step inside those haunted halls anymore.

You were dying, love.

Your father had found your body
slumped against the cold stone façade
of the gardening shed, practically dead,
your breath raspy and your voice weak
as you call out to the general who left you behind to die.

You were going to die.

They sent you home with non-skid socks and narcotics
and told your parents to dope you up, tuck you in,
and wait until you pissed yourself for one last time.

I prayed for you, wept for you,
I spent the morning on my knees for you
calling out to a god I didn't even believe in
because I thought maybe you did
and I could put in a good word for you
so that you wouldn't go to hell.

                  I didn't think you were going to hell—

you were too nice, caring, loving, gentle,
hold-me-and-keep-me-warm-because-you-love-me
kind of special—
but I was scared you would get caught in the crossfire
and end up in the hellfire
and I didn't want to be the one responsible.

The morning was dismal, and I'd be lying
if I said I didn't get hit by a stray bullet or two
while mourning you
and wishing that it could be me instead,
lying in that bed, waiting, paralyzed,
wishing that death would come to take me home
and put one more set of angel wings in the sky.

Wanted

I'm perpetually
looking
for that special someone
who can ruin me
in a way
nobody
has yet
to accomplish.

Reminiscing

We went to a fairy garden once.

It was beautiful—
all the little gnomes and fairy figurines
were perched among the rocks,
tiny houses and churches and school buildings
mingled with the hydrangea and marigolds—
the marbles scattered throughout the pebbles
glittered in the sun like tiny droplets of magic;

they shone just like my mother's eyes
when my father would bring her roses
from the shop down the street.

The roses in the fairy garden
looked just like my mother's favorites:
delicate, with deep pink centers
that faded to a light blush around the petal's edge.

It's memories like this—
the warmth of your breath against my ear,
the thick wool of my sweater sleeves covering my wrists,
the soft hum of a dragonfly's wings flying past our faces—
it's the memories like this that I want to hold on to forever,
to freeze in time, to cherish and love
and never let go of.

But I know the haze of the long days is setting in,
battlefield fatigue and a head full of smoke
from cannons that never seem to hit their targets—

I'm going to lose that fairy garden one day.

All the marigolds will wither and die,
and the roses will be taken prisoner
in a world full of battles and war crimes.

And while I hope that day is years away,
I'm already starting to lose
the hum of the dragonfly's wings
and I find myself studying pictures of your eyes
as if I can somehow burn their sparkle into my memory
before I wake up and can no longer remember
what they look like.

Sour Stomach

Some nights the taste of your smile
lingers on my tongue,
the sweetness I had once come to love
is now bitter, an acquired taste;
it's a luxury so few are lucky enough to try,
and yet I've tried so hard
to purge my palate of your name
a thousand times.

Most nights my taste buds
still cling to your initials;
most nights my breath still smells
like that peppermint gum you used to chew.

And I know they say peppermint
is the best cure for a stomachache,
but this nausea has settled in deep
and there's not enough tea in this world
to soothe my pain.

Dissociation

My memories are hazy
as if I'm watching myself
through clouded glass.

It's as if I've forgotten
how it felt to be alive.

In the Morning

I'll see you in the morning, he said.

In the morning meant sometime after the sun
swept sleepiness from the sky
and settled high above the clouds.

In the morning meant after the moon
slipped down behind the mountainside
and the last of the stars faded away.

In the morning meant waking up
to the sweet smell of magnolia trees
drifting in on the sultry breeze—

In the morning always meant
that he would wait for me to fall asleep
so his smile would be the first and last thing
that I would see.

I'll see you in the morning, he said,
but when I threw back my duvet and slid out of bed,
there was dust on the stool
where he always sat to read while he waited for me.

I'll see you in the morning,
but nobody was sitting in the kitchen.

Nobody was fiddling with the radio
to catch the scores of last night's ball game.

Nobody was stirring two sugars and a splash of milk
into a mug of cheap-tasting coffee.

Nobody was sitting with the morning paper
and a plate of eggs, over easy—

I wish that this would be over easy.

This grief, this pain,
this perpetually exhausting waiting game
where I keep reheating the same cup of tea
while I sit and weep quietly,
hoping he'd come back to me.

I'll see you in the morning, he said,
but I'm still waiting for morning to come.

Body

There are days where this body
disgusts me
pains me makes
me feel as though every breath
is fueling flames of anger and fear

and there are days
where I'd love to
strip the skin from my bones
and peel away
every muscle fiber
and sinew
just to start anew

but I'm not sure I'd know
what to do with hands
that never held you
with eyes
that never saw you
with a tongue
that never spoke your name

I'm not sure
I'd know what to do
with a body
that never loved you
because then this world
just wouldn't be the same

Countdown to the End of Time

You said we'd never be apart, that we'd live together forever, and I was too
scared to not believe you.
Yesterday you said we will never die. Yesterday you said I love you. Yesterday
you asked me to marry
you, but I have always been scared of marriage. Why does the government
need to certify the love
we have for each other? Why does the government tell me that a man can be
legally
bound to the woman he plans to torture for the rest of his life? Why does
the government tell me that they can't recognize the love I have for the man
who saved my life? Why does the government refuse to recognize my life?
You
always told me not to worry so much. You said time would take
care of things. After all, we'd have all the time in the
world, wouldn't we? Perhaps we are eternal, but only in memory,
in the way our spirit persists long beyond the grave.
I thought about that at your funeral, how your
soul only smiled on this Earth for nineteen
years; how I'm still searching for solace
and purpose within puddles of tears.
I am lost without you.
I am scared without
you. Where do
I go
now?

Insomnia

I'm tired.

I'm tired like I haven't slept in months,
like my body ran a marathon without me
and my brain is trying to catch up with my bones;
like I've spent an eternity chasing after my shadow
to try and find a place called home.

But what am I supposed to do
now that my shadow has eloped
and I have nowhere to be
except alone?

War Casualties

They read his obituary over the radio
around three in the afternoon;

do you think they'll read mine too?

Home

He wanted nothing more than to go home to a house with two floors, a garage, and enough room for an oversized easy chair in the den. He wanted the backyard to be big enough for a doghouse and a swing set, maybe a garden shed too, but not too big so that it wouldn't take more than forty-five minutes for him to cut the lawn.

He always said he'd never let me use the lawnmower.

He wanted kids, three or four of them, though I've mentioned I'd be fine with just two. He never said if he preferred sons or daughters, though he always dreamt of building a Victorian dollhouse, complete with powder-blue siding and slate shingles and little window boxes filled with tulips and geraniums.

He was good at things like that, good with his hands, and he could fix anything from a broken table leg to an aching heart. The only thing he couldn't fix, he said, was himself.

After he died, I couldn't help but wonder why he never tried harder.

And I know that's not for me to judge, not for me to scrutinize, but I can't help but wonder why God let him die if He really did exist.

He thought God did exist, sort of, believing in angels and Heaven and Hell; but he also believed in medicine and research, and I never understood how he could believe in something like God while also having faith in science.

Right before he died, he talked about going home, going home to some place in the sky with a big golden gate and where everything was shimmery and white. I asked him if he'd have a garage in heaven, and he said he might. He said he might even get a white picket fence if he was lucky.

I told him I knew he'd be lucky.

I'm not sure where he ended up once he died, where his mind and soul went to seek peace after his coffin was lowered into the ground, but I know that he got his easy chair, wherever it may be, and I know that he has a matching one waiting there for me.

Acknowledgements

Writing this book has been one of the most challenging feats that I've ever tackled, and it wouldn't have been possible without the help of my best friend, Sarah Humphrey. She has been by my side through every up and down, every curveball, and every bump along the way. She's the one who pushes me when I want to give up, and I'm incredibly blessed to have her endless love and support.

I'm also eternally grateful to Brandy Detwiler, Emily Derstine, Liz Gipe, and Jen Hesse for always being there to read every draft of every poem I write. They always know the right advice to give, questions to ask, and are never afraid to tell me exactly what needs to be said, even if I don't want to hear it.

I wouldn't have made it to where I am today without the fantastic teachers and mentors who have helped me learn, grow, and overcome every obstacle in my way. To Arie Ebaugh, Katie Anderson, Lisa Gates, Rick Worley, Jim Martini, Grant Moore, Carmine Sarracino, Rick and Wendy Fellinger, Tara Goodrich, Rob Spence, Nick Curry, Suzanne Webster, John Rohrkemper, and Suzanne Biever-Grodzinski, thank you for taking the time to teach me everything I needed to know in order to succeed in both writing and life.

I am forever indebted to my family and their endless love and support for everything I do. To my amazing parents, Mike and Lisa: thank you for always being there for every success, every failure, and all the questionable decisions in between, even when things make no sense to you whatsoever.

To my brother, Brian, and my sisters, Haylie and Allison: thank you for being the best cheerleaders, sidekicks, ninjas, and partners in crime I could have asked for. You make me so incredibly proud to be your big brother.

To my aunt, Jen, and my grandparents, Dan and Tammy: thank you for opening up your home and giving me a place to stay. You gave this book a place to grow, and I am eternally grateful for that.

To my grandparents, Cathy and Steve: thank you for always encouraging me to never stop learning. Every field trip, adventure, and journey to a new place inspired me to keep seeking out opportunities to learn and grow. I will forever cherish the memories of these trips.

To Becky, Jeremy, and Celina: thank you for being the best aunt, uncle, and cousin I could have ever asked for. Your unconditional love, support, and tolerance of my terrible sense of humor has carried me so far in life. I don't know where I would be without you.

And to my second mom, Krista Deemer: thank you for welcoming me into your life and showing me that family comes in many shapes and sizes. You have shown me love when I needed it the most and have helped me learn so much about myself.

I would also like to thank my editor, Emma Knight, and cover designer, Sam Shotzberger, for being amazing friends and for helping this book be the best it could possibly be. And to Kennedy Champitto and Sarah Caro of Nymeria Publishing, to whom I am beyond grateful for having faith in my work and giving this book a home. Without you, my dreams would still be dreams and I never would have brought my writing to life.

Finally, I owe a tremendous amount of gratitude to all those who have been along for the ride since the very beginning: Kaedy Masters, Gabe Mutschler, Samantha Seely, Anna Byriel, Grace Gibson, Aprille Mohn, Devon Moravec, Kennedy Gilbert, Amy Frasch, Erin Vago, Courtney Comer, Mallory Forney, Alex Smith, Ashlee Reick, Mika Cook, Salem Moser, Andrew Boeren, Amelia Reep, and Harley Rife.

As the saying goes, "it takes a village," and this book wouldn't have been possible without all of the love and support from each and every one of you.

From the bottom of my heart, thank you.

CPSIA information can be obtained
at www.ICGtesting.com
Printed in the USA
LVHW041035290622
722206LV00005B/89

9 798985 157239